A Guide for Using

By the Great Horn Spoon!

in the Classroom

Based on the novel written by Sid Fleischman

This guide written by **Michael H. Levin M.A.**

Teacher Created Resources, Inc.
6421 Industry Way
Westminster, CA 92683
www.teachercreated.com
ISBN: 978-1-55734-528-8
©*1996 Teacher Created Resources, Inc.*
Reprinted, 2008
Made in U.S.A.

Illustrated by
Keith Vasconcelles

Cover Art by
Nancee McClure

Table of Contents

Introduction

A good book can touch our lives like a good friend. Within its pages are words and characters that can inspire us to achieve our highest ideals. We can turn to it for companionship, recreation, comfort, and guidance. It can also give us a cherished story to hold in our hearts forever.

In *Literature Units,* great care has been taken to select books that are sure to become good friends!

Teachers who use this literature unit will find the following features to supplement their own valuable ideas.

- Sample Lesson Plans

- Pre-reading Activities

- A Biographical Sketch and Picture of the Author

- A Book Summary

- Vocabulary Lists and Suggested Vocabulary Activities

- Chapters grouped for study, with each section including:
  - *quizzes*
  - *hands-on projects*
  - *cooperative learning activities*
  - *cross-curriculum connections*
  - *extensions into the reader's own life*

- Post-reading Activities

- Book Report Ideas

- Research Ideas

- A Culminating Activity

- Three Different Options for Unit Tests

- Bibliography

- Answer Key

We are confident this unit will be a valuable addition to your lesson planning. Through the use of our ideas, we hope that your students will increase their circle of book "friends."

Sample Lesson Plan

Lesson 1

- Introduce and complete some or all of the pre-reading activities found on page 5.
- Decorate your room. (page 6)
- Read "About the Author" with your students. (page 7)
- Introduce the vocabulary list for Section 1. (page 9)

Lesson 2

- Read Chapters 1 through 3. As you read, place the vocabulary words in the context of the story and discuss their meanings.
- Do a vocabulary activity. (page 10)
- Draft and respond. (page 12)
- Work on sea routes. (pages 13 and 14)
- Choose a route to California. (page 13)
- Begin "Reading Response Journals." (page 15)
- Administer the Section 1 quiz. (page 11)
- Introduce the vocabulary list for Section 2. (page 9)

Lesson 3

- Read Chapters 4 through 7. Place the vocabulary words in context and discuss their meanings.
- Do a vocabulary activity. (page 10)
- Draw a picture from the story. (page 17)
- Learn about longitude and latitude. (page 18)
- Sing some songs from the period of the novel. (page 19)
- Consider having a butler. (page 20)
- Administer Section 2 quiz. (page 16)
- Introduce the vocabulary list for Section 3. (page 9)

Lesson 4

- Read Chapters 8 through 11. Place the vocabulary words in context and discuss their meanings.
- Do a vocabulary activity. (page 10)
- Cook some regional dishes. (page 22)
- Discuss problems of discovery gold. (page 23)
- Learn about similies. (page 24)

- Find out what food cost during the Gold Rush. (page 25)
- Administer Section 3 quiz. (page 21)
- Introduce the vocabulary list for Section 4. (page 9)

Lesson 5

- Read Chapters 12 through 15. Place the vocabulary words in context and discuss their meanings.
- Do a vocabulary activity. (page 10)
- Pan for gold (page 27)
- Create the perfect meal. (page 28)
- Find out about diseases. (page 29)
- Write a postcard. (page 30)
- Administer Section 4 quiz. (page 26)
- Introduce the vocabulary list for Section 5. (page 9)

Lesson 6

- Read Chapters 16 through 18. Place the vocabulary words in context and discuss their meanings.
- Do a vocabulary activity. (page 10)
- Create a new town (page 32)
- Figure out phrases. (page 33)
- Find out what areas produce gold today. (page 34)
- Think about what makes a family. (page 35)
- Administer Section 5 quiz. (page 31)

Lesson 7

- Discuss any questions your students have about the story. (page 36)
- Assign book report and research activity. (pages 37 and 38).
- Begin work on one or more culminating activities. (page 39-42)

Lesson 8

- Administer Unit Tests: 1, 2, and/or 3. (pages 43, 44, and 45)
- Discuss the test answers and possibilities.
- Discuss the student's enjoyment of the book.
- Provide a list of related reading for your students. (page 46)

Before the Book

Before you begin reading *By the Great Horn Spoon!* with your students, do some pre-reading activities to stimulate interest and enhance comprehension. Here are some activities that might work for your class.

1. Predict what the story might be about just by hearing the title.

2. Predict what the story might be about just by looking at the cover illustration.

3. Discuss other books by Sid Fleischman that students may have heard about or read.

4. Answer these questions:

    • Are you interested in:

      —stories about children who have to be heroic?

      —stories about the Old West?

      —stories with adventure and life or death struggles?

      —stories dealing with young persons having experiences that make them grow up?

      —stories that show a young person capable of making important decisions and taking action?

      —stories that have funny and unusual happenings?

    • Why might a young boy or girl need to leave home to help the family?

    • How can unusual occurrences change a young person's life?

    • What might it be like to have a butler who is always there to help you but also watches how you are acting?

    • What is it like being in a new and completely different environment?

5. Work in groups to create a factual and/or fictional story about a boy who leaves his home and has strange adventures.

6. Write descriptions or brainstorm ideas about what makes a person strong or courageous.

Before the Book *(cont.)*

There's Gold in That There Class!

Consider turning your classroom into a gold mine as you read *By the Great Horn Spoon!* Your students will enjoy the experience, and it will make a great introduction to the novel. The room will also be decorated if you want to invite parents for a presentation. Use some of the other ideas in this book to create an interesting presentation—songs (page 19), food (page 22), panning for gold (page 27), art work (pages 17, 30, 32) and displays of writing (pages 23, 30, 32, 40, 42).

Here's one way to make your room into a gold mine!

1. Cover the outside of your door in brown paper to represent the outside of the mine before digging.

2. Cover the areas above and below the chalkboard in black paper to represent the dark walls of the mine. The paper should be two to three feet (61 to 91 cm) wide. Depending on the configuration of your room, the black paper can start at the door and wrap around the room to the chalkboard.

3. The gold vein can run immediately above and below the board. Using a permanent gold or yellow color marker, carefully color aluminum foil gold. Attach aluminum foil to the black paper.

4. You can paint a few nuggets and put them in various places along the black paper.

5. Place artifacts—pie tins (gold panning bowls), shovels, picks, claim certificates, etc.—around the room.

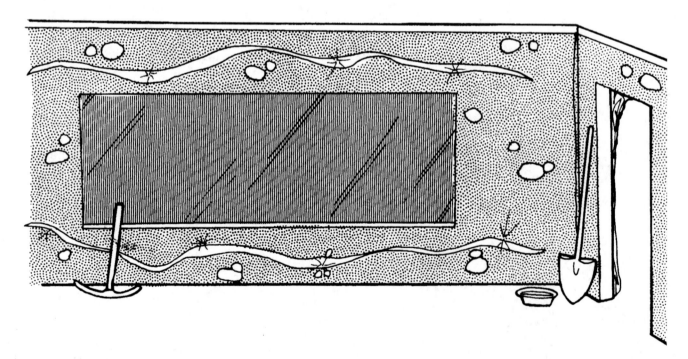

About the Author

Albert Sidney Fleischman was born on March 16, 1920, in Brooklyn, New York to Rueben and Sadie (Solomon) Fleischman. He attended San Diego State College (now University) and received a B.A. in 1949. He married Betty Taylor in 1942, and they have two daughters and a son.

Fleischman began his career as a professional magician. He traveled with a magic show in 1939. He was in the Navy from 1941-1945, serving as a yeoman on a destroyer escort in the Philippines, Borneo, and China. From 1949-1951 he worked for the *San Diego Daily Journal,* first as a reporter and then as an associate editor.

In 1951, Fleischman became a full-time writer. He has written over 50 books and screenplays. Although most of his books are for young people, he has written over 10 novels for adults.

Fleischman's success as a writer is evident in the many awards and honors he has received:

- *Mr. Mysterious and Company* was the *New York Herald Tribune's* Children's Spring Book Festival Award Honor Book for 1962;

- *By the Great Horn Spoon!* received the Spur Award from the Western Writers of America, the Southern California Council on Literature for Young People Award, and the Boy's Clubs of America Junior Book Award, all in 1964;

- *McBroom Tells the Truth* received the Lewis Carroll Award in 1969;

- *Humbug Mountain* was a National Book Award finalist and received the Boston Globe-Horn Book Award for fiction, both in 1979;

- *The Whipping Boy* received the Newbery Award in 1987.

When asked about how he writes, Sid Fleischman had this to say:

> *I compose very slowly. My first draft is a kind of finished draft. I... chip out each sentence with care...I will stay with that page until I think it is as good as I can make it. On some days I will get only one page of work finished; on other days, five or six.*

(**Something About the Author,** Edited by Anne Commire, Gale Research, Detroit, 1973 and 1989.)

By the Great Horn Spoon!

by Sid Fleischman

(Little, Brown and Company, 1963, 1988)
(Available in Canada and UK from Little Brown Ltd.; AUS, Penguin Aus)

By the Great Horn Spoon! takes place during the California Gold Rush in January, 1849. (Gold was discovered at Sutter's Mill about one year before.) Jack Flagg is a twelve-year old orphan who decides to run away to California and find gold in order to save the family home and support his Aunt Arabella and his sisters, Constance and Sarah. Jack and the elegant butler, Praiseworthy, are forced to stow away on the *Lady Wilma* when their passage money is stolen on the crowded docks of Boston Harbor. Once at sea, Jack and Praiseworthy meet Captain Swain, the "Wild Bull of the Seas," who is engaged in a race to San Francisco with the *Sea Raven*.

Praiseworthy, with Jack's help and the use of Good Luck, a pig, is able to deduce the identity of the "cut-purse" who stole their money. Cut-Eye Higgins is sent to the coal furnaces. Jack thinks Praiseworthy is able to do just about anything and wishes that the butler would be less formal with him and act more like a friend.

The *Sea Raven* beats their ship into the harbor of Callao, Peru, and leaves with all the coal to be had. However, this turns out to be the undoing of the Sea Raven. It is now too heavy, and at Praiseworthy's suggestion, the *Lady Wilma* burns the lumber in her hold and sails into San Francisco to win the race.

In the gold fields, Jack and Praiseworthy are befriended by a miner who shows them how to dig and allows them to work on his claim. Jack, who found a picture of his aunt in Praiseworthy's carpetbag, tells the butler he ought to ask Aunt Arabella to marry him. Praiseworthy feels he does not have the social standing to consider this and reluctantly dismisses the thought.

Jack and Praiseworthy run into Cut-Eye Higgins again just as the thief is about to be hanged. They save him for a bit, but are forced to dig his grave. While digging, they discover gold and quickly stake their claim. They board the riverboat *Rich Men*. But on the way back to San Francisco, the boiler of the riverboat explodes, and their gold dust ends up on the bottom of the bay.

However, once again fate comes to their rescue. San Francisco is overrun with rats. As Jack and Praiseworthy search the *Lady Wilma* for Captain Swain, they realize the cats on board have multiplied many times. They sell the cats to San Francisco merchants and are once again rich. But their biggest surprise is still to come. Aunt Arabella, Constance, and Sarah arrive from Boston. They are all reunited. Praiseworthy feels California is less formal than Boston and asks Arabella to be his wife. She accepts, and Jack gets the family he has always wanted.

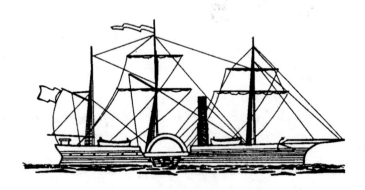

Vocabulary Lists

On this page are vocabulary lists which correspond to each sectional grouping of chapters. Vocabulary activity ideas can be found on page 10 of this book.

Section 1
Chapters 1-3

slake	dire	lurch	penetrate	clamor
imperative	cholera	baffle(d)	despicable	scoundrel
suspicion	anxious	fierce	balance	rogue
undaunted	dispirited	molting	dispirited	oozed

Section 2
Chapters 4-7

latitude(s)	banshee	tarry	exotic	guava
horrendous	impending	yarn	inclement	Patagonia
monotony	becalmed	languished	ration(ed)	stalwart

Section 3
Chapters 8-11

frigate	dilemma	amble(d)	hospitality	courteous
necessity	obliged	lunatic	undertaker	awesome
patience	exasperated	jostling	imposter	extractor

Section 4
Chapters 12-15

elated	peer(ing)	exaggerate(d)	notoriety	bedrock
petrified	elegant	emerge(d)	idly	fisticuffs

Section 5
Chapters 16-18

festivities	heinous	dispatch	interfere	reprieve
cantankerous	exuberance	savor	invincible	vigilant

Vocabulary Activity Ideas

You can help your students learn and retain the vocabulary in *By the Great Horn Spoon!* by providing them with interesting vocabulary activities. Here are some ideas to try.

- People of all ages like to make and solve puzzles. Ask your students to make their own **Crossword Puzzles** or **Word Search Puzzles** using the vocabulary words from the story.

- Challenge your students to a **Vocabulary Bee!** This is similar to a spelling bee, but in addition to spelling each word correctly, the game participants must also correctly define the words.

- Play **Vocabulary Concentration.** The goal of this game is to match vocabulary words with their definitions. Divide the class into groups of 2-5 students. Have students make two sets of the cards, the same size and color. On one set have them write the vocabulary words. On the second set have them write the definitions. All cards are mixed together and placed face down on a table. A player picks two cards. If the pair matches the word with its definition, the player keeps the cards and takes another turn. If the cards don't match, they are returned to their places face down on the table, and another player takes a turn. Player must concentrate to remember the locations of the words and their definitions. The game continues until all matches have been made. This is an ideal activity for free exploration time.

- Have your students practice their writing skills by creating sentences and paragraphs in which multiple vocabulary words are used correctly. Ask them to share their **Compact Vocabulary** sentences and paragraphs with the class.

- Ask your students to create paragraphs which use the vocabulary words to present **History Lessons** that relate to the time period of the novel.

- Challenge your students to use a specific vocabulary word from the story at least **10 Times in One Day.** They must keep a record of when, how, and why the word was used.

- As a group activity, have students work together to create an **Illustrated Dictionary** of the vocabulary words.

- Play **20 Clues** with the entire class. In this game, one student selects a vocabulary word and gives clues about this word, one by one, until someone in the class can guess the word.

- Play **Vocabulary Charades.** In this game, vocabulary words are acted out.

You probably have many more ideas to add to this list. Try them! See if experiencing vocabulary on a personal level increases your students' vocabulary interest and retention.

What Do You Know?

Answer the following questions about Chapters 1, 2, and 3.

1. Why do Jack and Praiseworthy become stowaways?

   _____

   _____

2. Why does Jack want to go to the gold fields and strike it rich?

   _____

   _____

3. Why does Captain Swain want his ship, the *Lady Wilma*, to beat the *Sea Raven* to San Francisco?

   _____

   _____

4. What job does the Captain order Praiseworthy to do?

   _____

   _____

5. When the Captain says Jack is to be a ship's boy, what does Jack say?

   _____

   _____

6. What does Praiseworthy put on Good Luck, the pig, in order to uncover the "cut-purse"? What happens then?

   _____

   _____

7. Where were the banknotes discovered in Higgin's cabin?

   _____

   _____

8. Describe two of the four passengers who shared the cabin with Jack and Praiseworthy.

   _____

   _____

9. What city will be the ship's first port of call? What country is this city in?

   _____

   _____

10. When the *Lady Wilma* passes a ship that has been becalmed for a week, what does their captain ask Captain Swain to do? How long does this take?

   _____

   _____

Peer Response

In this exercise you are going to get some feed-back on your writing from two other people in class.

On another sheet of paper, take 15 minutes to write a first draft on one of the following topics which are related to *By the Great Horn Spoon!* Do not title your piece.

- • When you choose a friend, what qualities do you look for?

- • If you suddenly found $5,000, how would you spend it?

- • If you could live anywhere in the world, where would it be? Why?

Break into groups of three. Pass your paper to the person on your right. Take the paper from the person on your left. Read that draft and then fill in the chart below.

Writer: _____   Reader: _____

I like ...	I would like to know more about ...
I suggest ...	A good title for this piece is ...

Fold down the sheet so only the empty chart below shows. Pass it and the draft to your right.

Writer: _____   Reader: _____

I like ...	I would like to know more about ...
I suggest ...	A good title for this piece is ...

Pass this paper and the draft to its owner. Read the different responses from your peers. Consider what they had to say. Revise your paper in anyway you think would make it better. Title your paper.

Sea Routes

Jack and Praiseworthy made the trip from Boston to San Francisco by traveling around the tip of South America. This was not the only way to get there from the East.

Some gold seekers took a boat to Panama (as Cut-Eye Higgins did). Once there, they had to travel first by steamboat, then bongo (a native raft), and finally on a mule in order to get to the Pacific side of the Isthmus. Upon arrival, it often took weeks to get on another ship that would take them the rest of the way to California.

Others took the overland route, as the undertaker Jonas T. Fletcher of Hangtown did, traveling by covered wagon or horse cart across the mountains and deserts of the West.

Each way held adventures as well as dangers.

Part 1

If you were traveling to the gold fields as Jack did, which way would you have wanted to go? State your reasons telling why you chose this way to the gold fields.

Part 2

On the map on page 14, find the following points along the routes, and then label them.

Atlantic Ocean	Sutter's Fort
Pacific Ocean	Brazil
North America	Rio de Janiero
South America	Tierra del Fuego
Central America	Straits of Magellan
Boston	Chile
New York City	Valparaiso
San Francisco	Peru
Sacramento	Callao
St.Joseph and Independence *(Missouri)*	Galapagos Islands
The Oregon Trail	Panama City
The California Trail	Equator

Map of Sea Routes

Reading Response Journals

One great way to insure that the reading of *By the Great Horn Spoon!* becomes a personal experience for each student is to include the use of Reading Response Journals in your plans. In these journals, students can be encouraged to respond to the story in a number of ways. Here are a few ideas.

- Tell them that the purpose of the journal is to record their thoughts, ideas, observations, and questions as they read *By the Great Horn Spoon!*

- Provide students with, or ask them to suggest topics from the story that would stimulate writing. Here are a few examples from the chapters in Section 1:

  — Traveling on a ship in the 1800's was a very different kind of transportation than riding in a car or on an airplane. What special problems do you think passengers might have had?

  — Some readers might say that Jack had a strong spirit of adventure. What might this mean?

  — Being an orphan and feeling lonely, Jack wanted to be real friends with Praiseworthy. Why is it important for people to feel they belong to a group and are not alone in the world? Why do most people want to have a family whose members care about one another?

- After the reading of each chapter, students can write one or more new things they learned in the chapter.

- Ask students to draw their responses to certain events or characters in the story, using blank pages in their journals.

- Tell students that they may use their journals to record "diary-type" responses that they want to enter.

- Encourage students to bring their journal ideas to life! Ideas generated from their journal writing can be used to create plays, debates, stories, songs, and art displays.

- Give students quotes from the novel and ask them to write their own responses. (Make sure to do this before you go over the quotations in class.) In groups, they could list the different ways students can respond to the same quote.

Allow students time to write in their journals daily.

- Personal reflections will be read by the teacher, but no corrections or letter grades will be assigned. Credit is given for effort, and all students who sincerely try will be awarded credit. If a grade is desired for this type of entry, grade according to the number of journal entries completed. For example, if five journal assignments were made and the student conscientiously completes all five, then he or she receives an "A".

- Non-judgmental teacher response should be made as you read journals to let the students know you are reading and enjoying their journals. Here are some types of responses that will please your journal writers and encourage them to write more.

  — "You have really found what's important in the story!"

  — "You write so clearly, I almost feel as if I am there."

  — "If you feel comfortable, I'd like you to share this with the class. I think they'll enjoy it as much as I did."

What Do You Know?

Answer the following questions about Chapters 4, 5, 6, and 7.

1. On the back of this paper, write a one paragraph summary of the major events that happened in these four chapters. Then complete the rest of the questions on this page.

_____

_____

2. Why did Jack worry about Sunday dinners?

_____

_____

3. What did Jack and Praiseworthy buy in Rio de Janeiro that they never saw in Boston?

_____

_____

4. When "Cut-Eye Higgins" took the small stern ship, what did he steal from one of the passengers?

_____

_____

5. What did "Cut-Eye" take unexpectedly from the ship? Why was Jack happy about this?

_____

_____

6. As the ship moved further south to the tip of South America, why did the weather turn cold?

_____

_____

7. Why is Tierra del Fuego called "land of fire?"

_____

_____

8. Why did Captain Swain go through the dangerous Straits of Magellan instead of around Cape Horn?

_____

_____

9. How did Jack solve the problem of rotting potatoes and dry grape cuttings?

_____

_____

10. How did Praiseworthy's suggestion help the *Lady Wilma* to win the race?

_____

_____

Lady Wilma

The *Lady Wilma* plays an important role in *By the Great Horn Spoon!* Finish this picture of "her" anyway you wish. Some ideas: Picture the ship going through the rough waters of the Straits of Magellan. Picture the ship dropping anchor in San Francisco or Rio de Janeiro. Picture the becalmed ship on the wide Pacific. Don't forget to print *Lady Wilma* on her bow.

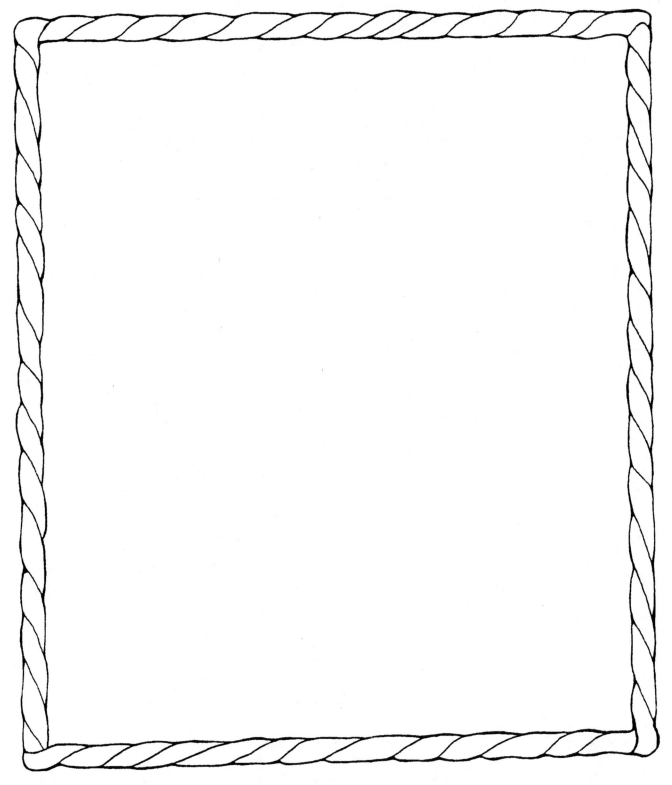

Latitude and Longitude

As the *Lady Wilma* moved toward Tierra del Fuego, it sailed into the Southern Latitudes. What does this mean? Latitude lines, which run west to east, and longitude lines, running from north to south, are imaginary lines that divide the earth. Sometimes called meridian lines, they divide the earth into sections and measure the distances from one area to another. Look at a world map to see the major latitude and longitude lines.

Latitude lines measure distances north and south of the equator. The equator is marked O degrees. The latitude lines north of the equator are marked ° N (degrees north) and the latitude lines south of the equator are marked ° S (degrees south).

Longitude lines measure distances west and east of the prime meridian. These imaginary lines run through Greenwich (pronounced Gren'ich) in England. The prime meridian divides the world into east and west longitudes. The longitude lines east of the prime meridian are marked ° E (degrees east) and those longitude lines west of the prime meridian are marked° W (degrees west).

The map of California below shows the latitude and longitude lines that divide the state. Use the map to answer these questions.

Which large city is near:

1. 34° N, 118° W?

   _____

2. 38° N, 122° W?

   _____

3. 33°N, 117°W?

   _____

Which small city is near:

4. 37° N, 122° W?

   _____

5. 37°N, 120°W?

   _____

6. 38° N, 121° W?

   _____

7. 35° N, 117° W?

   _____

8. 34° N, 117° W?

   _____

Which National Park, Monument, or Lake is near:

9. 37° N, 119° W?

   _____

10. 39° N, 120° W?

    _____

11. 38° N, 120° W?

    _____

12. 36° N, 117° W?

    _____

Songs of the Gold Rush

Every period of history has its special songs. Stephen Foster, America's most famous song writer of the nineteenth century wrote many of his compositions around the time of the California Gold Rush. Two of the most famous melodies, "Oh, Susanna" (1848) and "Camptown Races" (1850) provided enjoyment for the miners with an appropriate change of lyrics. Enjoy singing them to the familiar tunes!

"Oh, Susanna"

I come from dear old Boston with a washbowl on my knee,
I'm going to California the gold dust for to see.
It rained all night the day I left, the weather it was dry,
The sun so hot I froze to death, dear brother, don't you cry.

> Oh, Cal-i-for-ny
>
> O-That's the land for me! *(CHORUS)*
>
> I'm going to Sacramento
>
> With a washbowl on my knee.

I jumped aboard the largest ship and traveled on the sea,
And every time I thought of home, I wished it wasn't me!
The vessel reared like any horse that had of oats a wealth,
I found it wouldn't throw me, so I thought I'd throw myself! *(CHORUS)*
I thought of all the pleasant times we've had together here,
And I thought I ought to cry a bit, but I couldn't find a tear,
The pilot's bread was in my mouth, the gold dust in my eye,
And I thought I'm going far away, dear brother, don't you cry. *(CHORUS)*
I soon shall be in Frisco and there I'll look around,
And when I see the gold lumps there, I'll pick them off the ground.
I'll scrape the mountains clean, my boys, I'll drain the rivers dry,
A pocketful of rocks bring home, so brother, don't you cry.

* washbowl-pan that the gold miners used to separate the gold from the sand

"Camptown Races"

A bully ship and a bully crew
> Dooda, dooda,
A bully mate and a captain too,
> Dooda, dooda, day

Then blew ye winds hi-oh
For Cal-i-for-ny-o,
There's plenty of gold so I've been told
On the banks of the Sacramento.
Oh around Cape Horn we're bound to go,
> Dooda, dooda,
> **(CHORUS)**

Around Cape Horn through the sleet and snow,
> Dooda, dooda, day
> **(CHORUS)**

Oh around Cape Horn in the month of May
> Dooda, dooda,
> **(CHORUS)**

Oh around Cape Horn is a very long way,
> Dooda, dooda, day.
> **(CHORUS)**

Ninety days to Frisco Bay,
> Dooda, dooda,
Ninety days is darn good pay,
> Dooda, dooda, day
> **(CHORUS)**

I wish to God I'd never been born,
> Dooda, dooda,
To go a-sailin' round Cape Horn,
> Dooda, dooda, day
> **(CHORUS)**

To the Sacramento we're bound away,
> Dooda, dooda.
To the Sacramento's a heck of a way,
> Dooda, dooda, day.
> **(CHORUS)**

Having a Butler

As you know, Praiseworthy is a butler. The job of a butler is to help his employer do anything that needs to be done. Suppose you had a butler to help you. Consider this as you answer the following.

1. What would you most like your butler to do for you each day?

   _____

   _____

   _____

   _____

2. A butler often helped his employer dress. Would you like someone to pick out your clothes and help you get dressed? Why or why not?

   _____

   _____

   _____

   _____

3. A butler was supposed to be near his employer at almost all times. Would you want someone to be near you all the time? What problems would this cause?

   _____

   _____

   _____

   _____

4. Choose a name for your butler that would show what sort of person he was. (Why is Praiseworthy a good name for this character in the novel?)

   _____

   _____

   _____

   _____

What Do You Know?

Answer the following questions about Chapters 8, 9, 10, and 11.

1. On the back of this paper, write a one paragraph summary of the major events that happened in these four chapters. Then complete the rest of the questions on this page.

   _____

   _____

2. Why does it take so long for the laundry to wash shirts?

   _____

   _____

3. Why does Quartz Jackson want Jack to save all of his whiskers?

   _____

   _____

4. What are some of the strange sounding names of the gold towns? Which one does Jack want to get to?

   _____

   _____

5. How much did Jack and Praiseworthy get for selling one pick and one shovel?

   _____

   _____

6. When a road agent yells, "...reach for the sky—or I'll send you there pronto," what does he mean?

   _____

   _____

7. Whose picture did Praiseworthy have in his carpetbag?

   _____

   _____

8. How was Praiseworthy able to knock the big road agent "fifteen feet up hill"?

   _____

   _____

9. How does a miner stake a claim?

   _____

   _____

10. What does Pitch-pine Billy do with Praiseworthy's umbrella?

    _____

    _____

Miner Recipes

Jack and Praiseworthy ate many new foods during their adventures in *By the Great Horn Spoon!* Below are recipes cooks might have served them.

Sourdough Flapjacks

The flavor of sourdough is associated with California and was common in many recipes during the Gold Rush era.

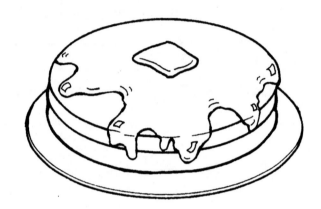

- 2 cups (480 mL) sourdough starter
- 4 cups (960 mL) warm water
- 1 tablespoon (15 mL) oil
- 1 teaspoon (5 mL) salt
- 4 tablespoons (60 mL) sugar
- 5 cups (1200 mL) flour
- 2 eggs
- ½ cup (120 mL) condensed milk
- 2 teaspoons (10 mL) baking soda

Mix starter, flour, and warm water the night before. Take out 2-3 cups to replenish starter. Add eggs, oil, and milk to what is left. Mix well. In a separate bowl, add salt, sugar, and baking soda. Sprinkle over dough and gently fold in. Let rise 3-4 minutes. Fry on hot griddle or pan. Serve immediately.

Dirt Cake

This is a modern adaptation of a cake the overland settlers brought with them from the East. It sounds sort of "gross" but it is fun to make and tastes even better. And remember—after spending hours digging in the hard earth, those miners often thought they were eating dirt!

- 1 large package of chocolate sandwich cookies
- 1-8 oz. (236 mL) package cream cheese
- ½ cup (120 mL) butter or margarine
- 1 cup (240 mL) powdered sugar
- 1 large carton prepared whipped topping
- Two 3.4 oz. (103 mL) packages instant vanilla pudding
- 3 cups (720 mL) milk
- 1 teaspoon (5 mL) vanilla

Crush cookies and put ½ cookie crumbs in 9 x 13-inch (23 cm x 33 cm) pan. Mix cream cheese and butter until smooth. Mix in sugar. Fold in topping. In a separate bowl, mix milk, pudding, and vanilla. Fold the mixtures together and pour into the pan over the crumbs. Spread remaining crumbs over top. Can be served frozen or chilled.

Gold Trouble

When gold was discovered at Sutter's Mill on January 24, 1848, John Sutter was upset. He knew other men would soon be coming to the area around his ranch. Sutter wanted nothing more than to live in peace and quiet. He loved the area around the Sacramento River and did not look forward to the changes gold would bring.

In 1848, the cry of gold signaled the chance for a miner's life to change forever by becoming wealthy. Today, people purchase lottery tickets with the hope of becoming millionaires. Sometimes, however, riches do not make a person happier.

In a group, consider the following questions. Discuss them in groups of three or four and then write down your thoughts and feelings.

1. How would finding gold change your life?

   _____

   _____

   _____

2. What would be the first thing you would change?

   _____

   _____

   _____

3. How might being rich be an advantage?

   _____

   _____

   _____

4. Can you think of ways that being very rich might be a problem?

   _____

   _____

   _____

5. Jack has a very specific reason for wanting to find gold. He wants to help Aunt Arabella save the family home. Who could you help if you suddenly became rich? Why would you want to help?

   _____

   _____

   _____

Similes

In *By the Great Horn Spoon!*, Sid Fleischman uses figurative language to help the reader get the "flavor" of the story. Figurative language helps the reader make connections between something new and something already known.

The most common type of figurative language in the novel is the simile. A simile compares one thing to another by using the words *as* or *like*. It helps better describe how something looks, feels, smells, tastes, or sounds by comparing the object to something else with which we are familiar.

Example from Chapter 10:

Finally the stage rounded a bend and the trail seemed to shoot up like a ladder. Going up the trail is compared to climbing a ladder. This helps the reader to realize how steep the trail was.

Praiseworthy, in his fury, struck like a bolt of lightning. The reader can understand how hard Praiseworthy hit the road agent because the author compares his swing to being hit by lightning.

Which of the following best explains the way Praiseworthy felt after the road agent took his coat?

A. Praiseworthy felt lost without his familiar coat.

B. Praiseworthy could not believe how bad he felt when his coat was taken.

C. Praiseworthy, unaccustomed to mere shirtsleeves, stood in the dust like a leopard suddenly deprived of his spots.

Of course, the last one is the best. Why? There is a comparison that the reader can understand. The coat is as important to Praiseworthy as skin would be to a leopard.

What are the following similes from chapter 10 and 11 comparing?

1. *...the driver's whip cracked in the air like rifle shots.*

   _____

2. *Far below, the pine trees looked to Jack like sharp green lances waiting to skewer them if they slipped.*

   _____

3. *The store shacks on both sides of the street were raised on wood pilings, like short legs, and looked as if they had just walked to town.*

   _____

Now it is time to write some of your own similes. Remember to compare the object given to you with some other more familiar object.

1. The weather was so cold it was as if _____

   _____

2. Tanya was so shy that when she spoke it was like _____

   _____

3. When Lee looked over the deep canyon, it seemed _____

   _____

Gold Rush Prices

When Jack and Praiseworthy arrived in San Francisco, they were amazed at how expensive everything was. This was due to the law of supply and demand. There were many people willing to spend just about anything to get what they wanted or needed, so the people selling raised prices as high as they wanted.

Below are prices certain items cost in San Francisco and in the gold fields during the years of 1848-1851. Compare them with prices these items cost today. Find out today's prices on your next trip to the market. Write them on the blank lines.

Gold Rush Days   **Today**

Bread	$1.00 (a slice)	_____	(a loaf)
Butter	$1.00 (⅛ lb.)	_____	(lb.)
Cheese	$8.00 (lb.)	_____	(lb.)
Onions	$1.50 (1b.)	_____	(lb.)
Salt Pork	$8.00 (1b.)	_____	(ham/lb.)
Sugar	$2.00 (lb.)	_____	(lb.)
Melon	$2-5.00 each	_____	(watermelon)
Flour	$1.00 (1b.)	_____	(lb.)
Beans	$1.00 (lb.)	_____	(lb)
Eggs	$2-3.00 each	_____	(dozen)
Sardines	$16.00 box	_____	(can)
Vinegar	$1.00 (½ pt.)	_____	(quart)
Candy	$.50 a piece	_____	(bar)

Extra: Add the amounts a miner would have paid for five items in California in 1849. Then find the cost of the same items today. What would be the difference in cost?

What Do You Know?

Answer the following questions about Chapters 12, 13, 14, and 15.

1. On the back of this paper, write a one-paragraph summary of the major events that happened in these chapters. Then complete the rest of the questions on this page.

_____

_____

2. What does it mean when someone "takes a hairbrush to you?"

_____

_____

3. Why does Praiseworthy think that Miss Arabella would not marry him?

_____

_____

4. How does Jack end up with a bushel of "neckties"?

_____

_____

5. Why do the miners "get in line" to buy the neckties?

_____

_____

6. Why does Praiseworthy think he can beat the Mountain Ox in a bare-knuckles fight?

_____

_____

7. What information did the miner with the toothache give to Jack and Praiseworthy?

_____

_____

8. Why was it fortunate for Jack that he fell down a coyote hole?

_____

_____

9. How does Jack know that the man who rescued him from the coyote hole was a road agent?

_____

_____

10. After Praiseworthy opens every inch of Cut-Eye's coat, what does he realize?

_____

_____

Pan for Gold

Try to pan for gold as Jack did in the novel. Use the directions below to bring the experience alive for your students.

Materials:

- gravel, gold spray paint, sand, pie tins, bucket, water.

Preparation:

Spray paint some small pieces of gravel. Bury the gold gravel in sand.

Directions:

1. Have each student take a small scoop of sand from the bucket and put it in a pie tin.

2. Place about 1/2 cup (120 mL) of water in the tin.

3. Over a sink or second bucket, have the student swirl the tin around in an orbital motion until the sand and water are washed out.

4. The gold gravel should remain.

Note: This is harder than it sounds. Students may have to practice a bit before they can do it successfully.

You might have students work in teams. The team with the most "gold" wins.

The Perfect Meal

Jamoka Jack got his name when Pitch-pine Billy thought the boy liked coffee. Most twelve-year olds would probably dislike coffee as much as Jack. However, some young people like to drink coffee.

Few of us have the same likes and dislikes when it comes to just about anything, especially food. In a group of three, fill in the following lists about food.

1. Make a list of the foods and drinks you dislike the most. Before you list it, at least two out of three in the group must agree the food is really "yucky."

    _____   _____

    _____   _____

    _____   _____

    _____   _____

2. Now it is time to list your group's favorite foods and drinks. Again, at least two of you must agree that each item is "yummy."

    _____   _____

    _____   _____

    _____   _____

    _____   _____

3. Now, create the perfect evening meal for your group. Here is where real teamwork will come into play. You must all agree that each item would be good to eat. You may not get your favorite food on your group's menu, but you should like whatever is chosen. Work together to create the perfect meal. Write your answer in the menu below.

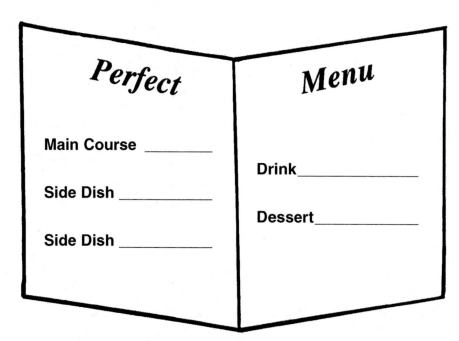

Perfect   Menu

Main Course _____

                              Drink_____

Side Dish _____

                              Dessert_____

Side Dish _____

Diseases of the Times

Many people who went to the gold fields caught diseases. Some that are uncommon today often caused death in the middle of the 19th century. Three of the most common were cholera (which claimed the lives of Jack's parents), yellow fever (which Dr. Buckbee caught in Panama), and scurvy (often a problem for sailors).

Using appropriate reference materials, fill in the following chart about these diseases.

	CHOLERA	**YELLOW FEVER**	**SCURVY**
Cause(s)			
Symptom(s)			
Damages which part(s) of body			
Cure(s)			
Prevention			
Other information			

Writing Home

Jack sends several letters home during the time he is away. It is important to let the people you love know what you are doing and how you are getting along.

Pretend you are away from home in some exotic location you have always wanted to visit. Write a postcard home. Be sure to make it personal—so it could have only been written by you. Include your address on the "back." Draw a picture of where you are "visiting" on the front.

Back (message/address)

Front (picture)

What Do You Know?

Answer the following questions about Chapters 16, 17, and 18.

1. On the back of this paper, write a one-paragraph summary of the major events that happened in these three chapters. Then complete the rest of the questions on this page.

2. How can a miner tell the difference between real gold and fool's gold by hitting them with a rock?

   _____

   _____

3. Why was Cut-Eye being hanged?

   _____

   _____

4. What happened as Jack and Praiseworthy dug a grave for Cut-Eye?

   _____

   _____

5. What parts of the Mountain Ox did Praiseworthy decide were his best targets?

   _____

   _____

6. What happened as the steamboat entered San Francisco Bay?

   _____

   _____

7. Why did Jack and Praiseworthy let their gold drop to the bottom of the bay?

   _____

   _____

8. How were Jack and Praiseworthy able to make another fortune?

   _____

   _____

9. Why did Aunt Arabella sell the house and sail to San Francisco with her two nieces?

   _____

   _____

10. Why is Jack so happy as the novel ends?

   _____

   _____

Create a Town

When the gold seekers reached the fields, there was often no town near the new strikes. Towns would be built in a matter of weeks.

Today, you suddenly find yourself in a new place that has no buildings at all. Furthermore, you are given the responsibility of creating a town. Answer the following questions and then draw a picture of your new town.

1. What would be some of the things you would have to consider first?

2. What sorts of places would new settlers in current times want to have?

3. What would be the five buildings or stores needed most? Why?

4. What types of buildings could wait a year or two until more settlers moved into the area? Why?

5. On a blank sheet of paper, draw a picture of your new town.

Colorful Speech

By the Great Horn Spoon! is full of examples of phrases people used in the middle of the 19th century. Sometimes it is easy to figure out what the characters are saying, and other times it can be difficult. Below in boldface are several phrases found in *By the Great Horn Spoon!* In a group, decide what could be a 20th century meaning for these 19th century phrases. (If you need some help, the person who said each statement and the chapter he said it in is noted.)

Example: Stuff and nonsense (Praiseworthy, Chapter 5)

That is ridiculous.

---

1. ***By the Great Horn Spoon!*** (Title)

   _____

2. *But I'll beat the Sea Raven,* **by grabs.** (Captain Swain, Chapter 1)

   _____

3. *Here's a lad* **with stuffings.** (Captain Swain, Chapter 1)

   _____

4. *I've known grizzly bears that were a mite friendlier than this* **Billy-be-hanged Cape Horn!** (Mountain Jim, Chapter 5)

   _____

5. ***Everything sky high.*** (Laundryman, Chapter 8)

   _____

6. *I ain't such a bad-looking gent...I'm just a* **mite growed over...** (Quartz Jackson, Chapter 8)

   _____

7. *The boy's* **panned himself some color.** (Quartz Jackson, Chapter 8)

   _____

8. *Shucks, looks like* **I wore a hole plumb through your washpan.** (Pitch-pine Billy, Chapter 11)

   _____

9. **Put hair on the boy's chest.** (Pitch-pine Billy, Chapter 11)

   _____

10. **It's no account. We don't stand on table manners** *out here.* (Pitch-pine Billy, Chapter 11)

   _____

Modern Gold Mining

Gold is still mined in California, as well as other states and parts of the world. Study the chart below and answer the questions about leading gold-mining states, Canadian provinces and territories. (The amounts of mined gold are measured in troy ounces. This is a system based on a pound of 12 ounces and an ounce of 480 grains.)

Amount of Gold Produced in a Year *(amounts are approximate)* 1 = 500,000 troy ounces	
Nevada	◯◯◯◯◯◯◯◯◯◯ 5, 000, 000 troy ounces
Ontario	◯◯◯◯◯ 2, 600, 000 troy ounces
Quebec	◯◯◌ 1, 200, 000 troy ounces
California	◯◯ 1, 000, 000 troy ounces
Utah	◯◌ 800, 000 troy ounces
South Dakota	◯ 500, 000 troy ounces
British Columbia	◌ 450, 000 troy ounces
Northwest Territories	◌ 4000, 000 troy ounces
Montana	◌ 350, 000 troy ounces
Washington	◌ 300, 000 troy ounces

1. How much more gold does Nevada mine than California? _____

2. a. How much gold does the leading province mine? _____

   b. How much does the lowest producing province mine? _____

3. How much gold does the lowest producing state mine?_____

4. How much do Montana and Washington mine together? _____

5. How much less gold does Utah mine than California?_____

6. How much more gold does Ontario mine than Quebec? _____

7. How much gold do British Columbia and Northwest Territories mine together? _____

8. If a state mined 4,000,000 troy ounces, draw how the nuggets would look on the chart.

   _____

9. If a province mined 6,000,000 troy ounces, draw how the nuggets would look on the chart.

   _____

10. Add the amounts of gold all the states mine. _____

Family

Jack wanted a family. At the end of the novel he is thrilled that he will have Praiseworthy as a father. Answer the following questions to better understand your own feelings on the subject of "family."

1. What makes a family? *(What is your definition of a family?)*

_____

_____

2. What makes a family get along?

_____

_____

3. What can make a family not get along?

_____

_____

4. How many children are best in making a family? Is there a certain number?

_____

_____

5. How about the siblings? Do you think it is better to have children of the same or opposite sex?

_____

_____

6. What problems do all families have?

_____

_____

7. What do you do if you feel your brother or sister gets better treatment from your parent(s)?

_____

_____

8. How can family members continue to care about each other?

_____

_____

Any Questions?

When you finished reading *By the Great Horn Spoon!*, did you have some questions that were left unanswered? Write them here.

_____

_____

_____

Then work in groups or by yourself to prepare possible answers for the questions you have asked above or those written below. When you have finished, share your ideas with the class.

- How old was Praiseworthy?

- What was the captain of the *Sea Raven* like?

- Will Monsieur Gaunt ever get his vineyard planted?

- Will Captain Swain ever command the new sailing ship?

- What finally happened to Cut-Eye Higgins?

- Will "Jamoka Jack" ever learn to like coffee?

- Will Jack and Praiseworthy sell all the cats that were on the *Lady Wilma*?

- Will Jack and Praiseworthy ever try to find their gold at the bottom of San Francisco Bay?

- Will Praiseworthy ever have to have a bare-knuckles fight again?

- Will they see Pitch-pine Billy or Quartz Jackson again?

- Will Jack ever go on a long ocean voyage again?

- Will Praiseworthy and Aunt Arabella have children of their own?

- How does Jack's life change now that his aunt and sisters are with him?

- Will Praiseworthy make a good father for Jack?

- Will Praiseworthy and Aunt Arabella adopt Jack, Sarah, and Constance?

- Where will the family live? In the gold fields? San Francisco?

- What will Praiseworthy do instead of being a butler?

- Will Aunt Arabella be happy living away from Boston?

- What will Jack's occupation be when he becomes an adult?

Book Report Ideas

There are numerous ways to report on a book once you have read it. After you have finished reading *By the Great Horn Spoon!*, choose one method of reporting on the book that interests you. It may be a way your teacher suggests, an idea of your own, or one of the ways that is mentioned below.

- **See What I Read?**

  This report is a visual one. A model of a scene from the story can be created, or a likeness of one or more of the characters from the story can be drawn or sculpted.

- **Time Capsule**

  This report provides people living at a future time with the reasons *By the Great Horn Spoon!* is such an outstanding book. It gives these "future" people reasons why it should be read. Make a time capsule type of design, and neatly print or write your reasons inside the capsule. You may wish to "bury" your capsule after you have shared it with your classmates. Perhaps one day someone will find it and read *By the Great Horn Spoon!* because of what you wrote!

- **Come To Life!**

  This report is one that lends itself to a group project. A size-appropriate group prepares a scene from the story for dramatization, acts it out, and relates the significance of the scene to the entire book. Costumes and props will add to the dramatization!

- **Into The Future**

  This report predicts what might happen if *By the Great Horn Spoon!* were to continue. It may take the form of a story in narrative or dramatic form, or a visual display.

- **Guess Who or What**

  This report is similar to "Twenty Questions." The reporter gives a series of clues about a character from the story in vague to precise, general to specific order. After all clues have been given, the identity of the mystery character must be deduced. (Use animal characters as well as human.) After the character has been guessed, the same reporter presents another "Twenty Clues" about an event in the story.

- **A Character Comes To Life!**

  Suppose one of the characters in *By the Great Horn Spoon!* came to life and walked into your home or classroom. This report gives a view of what this character sees, hears, and feels as he or she experiences the world in which you live.

- **Sales Talk**

  This report serves as an advertisement to "sell" *By the Great Horn Spoon!* to one or more specific groups. You decide on the group to target and the sales pitch you will use. Include some kind of graphics in your presentation.

- **Literary Interview**

  This report is done in pairs. One student will pretend to be a character in the story, steeped completely in the persona of his or her character. The other student will play the role of a television or radio interviewer, trying to provide the audience with insights into the character's personality and life. It is the responsibility of the partners to create meaningful questions and appropriate responses.

Research: Ship Terms

The *Lady Wilma* was a cross between the majestic clipper ships and the steam powered paddlewheelers. Shipbuilders and sailors have their own jargon or terms used to describe different parts of the ship. Learn about these terms. Most are mentioned in chapters 1-6 of *By the Great Horn Spoon!* See how many parts of the ship you can label on the diagram of the ship below.

sidewheels	keel	porthole
beam	forecastle (fo'c'sle)	bow
stern	capstan	riggings
bowsprit	crow's nest	top sails
hold	stern boat	galley
fore	aft	deck
jib	ratline	shroud
mast	yard (yardarms)	pilothouse
starboard	port	

One-Pager

A "one-pager" is a chance for you to draw or write your reaction to *By the Great Horn Spoon!*. It is yours to do whatever you want, as long as it relates to the novel. Use a separate sheet of paper—you will need to decide whether it should be all lined, have just a few lines, or be blank.

The only requirement is that your page has to have some color on it. If you don't want to draw, then put a colorful border around your writing.

Some suggestions—

- You can pick out a favorite quote and illustrate it with your own view of the characters. (See page 44 for a list of quotes.)

- You can draw a scene that the author described in words.

- You can draw the climactic scene of the novel.

- You can draw a scene that "occurs" before the action of the novel.

- You can draw a scene that "occurs" after the novel ends.

- You can draw a new book cover for the novel.

- You can write your feelings about the novel. For example, how does the novel relate to the real world?

- You can a write a review of the novel.

How the Town Got Its Name

Rough and Ready	You Bet	Ragtown
Last Chance	Bedbug	Sailor's Slide
SkunkGulch	Fiddletown	Shirt-Tail Camp
Shinbone Creek	Angels Camp	Red Dog
Poker Flat	Ten-Cent Gulch	Fair Play
Get-Up-And-Git	Dogtown	Total Wreck
Chucklehead Diggings	Salt Pork Ridge	Humbug Canyon

The towns of the Gold Rush had colorful names, and each one probably could "tell" a story about how it got it. However, since almost all are ghost towns now, it is difficult to find out how they got their names. Anyhow, it would be more fun to make your own stories.

Choose one of the town names and create a story of how it got its name. The story can be humorous or serious. It will be pure fiction, so make it as wild as the West was in 1849! Need an example? Here's one about the town Jack chose to dig near—Hangtown.

It was called No-Name Town when 10 hearty miners built a little cabin in the mountains 90 miles northeast of Sacramento. Almost as soon as they began digging, gold was found. Hundreds of people quickly moved into No-Name Town.

Before long there were little stores built and, of course, a hotel and numerous drinking establishments. The miners were hard working and rarely did any trouble develop. There were a few fights on Saturday night, but they were usually settled quickly. On Sundays the men wrote letters home and did their laundry, getting ready for the hard week ahead. By the afternoon on a sunny Sunday there were hundreds of red flannel shirts waving on clotheslines all over No-Name Town.

Three men rode into town one day early in 1849. They were not hard working miners. In fact, these men wanted to make their money by stealing other men's gold. They decided to take Big John's gold late on Friday night. But Big John had a big loner wolf he had trained to watch over his claim. The thieves got within 6 feet of the claim when the wolf attacked. There was such a commotion that Big John and his friends were there within a minute.

The robbers were sentenced to death on Saturday with the hanging to take place the next day. Every person in town wanted to be at the execution, so they did their laundry early that Sunday. Miners from other towns nearby began arriving. A group from Red Dog rode through No-Name Town and noticed all the red shirts flapping in the breeze. It was such a funny sight that they called it Hangtown—and that's how it got its name.

(Hangtown, by the way, was one of the few towns that still exist today. It was renamed Placerville, and has many buildings and sights left from the frontier days.)

Working Out Solutions

In Chapter 2, Praiseworthy and Jack (with Good Luck's help), are able to figure out who stole their money. Praiseworthy knows an answer to a problem can be found if a person thinks about it long enough.

In Chapter 6, Jack works out the problem of the spoiled potatoes and the drying grape cuttings. Jack, it seems, also has learned that even difficult problems have a solution.

Throughout the novel, the reader will see that Jack, and especially Praiseworthy, will never dismiss a situation as hopeless. They understand that the time for solving a problem will come as long as you continue to look for a solution.

In the following chapters, what are the problems facing characters in the book, and how do Praiseworthy and Jack solve them?

Part 1

1. *(Chapter 7)* Problem _____ _____ _____ Solution _____ _____ _____	3. *(Chapter 16)* Problem _____ _____ _____ Solution _____ _____ _____
2. *(Chapter 13)* Problem _____ _____ _____ Solution _____ _____ _____	4. *(Chapter 18)* Problem _____ _____ _____ Solution _____ _____ _____

Working Out Solutions *(cont.)*

Part 2

In groups of three or four, discuss how the following "impossible" situations can be worked out.

1. Suppose there was a thief in your classroom. A student recently had his lunch money taken during recess. How should the guilty party be found?

2. Five people want the lead in the class play which will be presented for parents at open house. How should the person be chosen so it will be fair to everyone?

3. No one wants to run for class president, but someone must be chosen. How do you go about having people run for the office?

4. Someone in class does not have enough money to go on the class trip which costs $10.00. How can the class provide money for this student without making him or her feel bad about "taking charity"?

Part 3

Even better than these examples would be a real life problem facing your class or school right now. Choose and discuss a current problem. Then brainstorm possible ways the problem can be solved. After the discussion, return to your desk and write out the problem clearly on the lines below and then describe the best solution.

_____

_____

_____

_____

_____

_____

_____

_____

_____

_____

Unit Test

Matching: Match the quote with the person who said it.

> Jack   Mountain Ox   Praiseworthy   Captain Swain
> Quartz Jackson   Pitch-pine Billy   Aunt Arabella   Cut-Eye Higgins

1. _____ *'It was time to rid ourselves of that house—of the past. It's like being free of a curse.*

2. _____ *'Ah Lee, go fry me up about two dozen more oysters. I'll be there in a minute—soon as I whip this Bullwhip fella.*

3. _____ *'By grabs, here's a lad with stuffings. He doesn't want an easy berth. Wants a man's job. All right, to the coal bunkers, both of you.*

4. _____ *'Why, look there! The boy's panned himself some color. I figured I scratched enough pay dirt into my beard to assay out at about $14 an ounce. Since I give you the whiskers and all—the gold is yours!'*

5. _____ *'Rio was too hot for me, you might say. So I lit out for Panama. Crossed the Isthmus by bongo boat and muleback—a whole parade of folks is getting to the Pacific that way. And looks like I beat you to California at that.*

6. _____ *'Nonsense. Spoiled the potatoes may be—but juicy they are, sir. Master Jack can attest to that. Why, they're like fat raindrops in brown skins.*

7. _____ *'You a friend of ol' Quartz! Why didn't you say so? Stay for dinner, hear. We'll have sowbelly-and-beans! I won't take no for an answer, hear! Now let's get our boots wet and I'll learn you how to pan.*

8. _____ *'I wish Aunt Arabella and Constance and Sarah were with us. But, of course, the gold country is no place for women and children.*

True or False: Write true or false next to each statement below.

1. _____ The money Higgins stole from Jack and Praiseworthy was found rolled up in cigars.

2. _____ Captain Swain takes the *Lady Wilma* around Cape Horn.

3. _____ Prices of items in San Francisco were cheaper than in Boston.

4. _____ Praiseworthy doesn't think Aunt Arabella would marry him because he is a butler.

5. _____ Jack and Praiseworthy discover gold while digging a grave for Cut-Eye Higgins.

Sequence: Number these events in the order they occurred in the story.

_____ The *Lady Wilma* beats the *Sea Raven* to San Francisco.

_____ The steamboat blows up in San Francisco Bay.

_____ Pitch-pine Billy teaches Praiseworthy to pan for gold using the butler's umbrella.

_____ Jack and Praiseworthy sell cats and make four hundred dollars.

_____ Jack and Praiseworthy meet Cut-Eye Higgins again on a stagecoach heading to the gold fields.

Paragraphs: Answer the following in paragraph form on the back of this sheet.

1. Discuss what lessons Jack learned about life as he traveled with Praiseworthy during the course of the novel.

2. Discuss why Jack wanted Praiseworthy to be more of a friend and father to him and less of a "butler."

Response

Explain the meaning of each of these quotations from *By the Great Horn Spoon!*.

Chapter 1:   *'By grabs, here's a lad with stuffings. He doesn't want an easy berth. Wants a man's job.'*

Chapter 2:   *'Nevertheless, I believe [the cut-purse] he's among your passengers like a fox among sheep.'*

Chapter 3:   *'I mean, if you weren't a butler, you wouldn't have to call me Master Jack as if we were at home. We're partners. You could call me Jack. Plain Jack.'*

Chapter 4:   *'Cape Horn lies ahead of us. It's a bad stretch of water... The wind comes howling in like banshees and the waves can batter a ship to splinters. No one will think less of you, Master Jack if you leave the* Lady Wilma *here at Rio.'*

Chapter 5:   *'You didn't see the fires of Tierra del Fuego—because they weren't to be seen.'*

Chapter 6:   *'It's the end of the race that counts.'*

Chapter 6:   *'I suggest that you buy Mr. Azariah Jones's eighteen barrels of potatoes. They're a bit spoiled, but a good bargain.'*

Chapter 7:   *'By grabs! I guess if there's anything heavier than a ton of bricks—it's a ton of coal!'*

Chapter 8:   *'Champagne'd be almost cheaper, gents... Unless you want to wait until next November. Prices come down when it rains.'*

Chapter 8:   *'Jack, young Jack a bit of sideburn is gettin' away in the breeze. Wouldn't want you to lose any.'*

Chapter 9:   *(Jonas T. Fletcher) 'Ain't that a fine-looking jipijapa hat he's got? Musta bought that in Panama. I come across the plains, myself. Clear from Missouri.'*

Chapter 10:   *'Throw down your rifle. The rest of you reach for the sky—or I'll send you there pronto.'*

Chapter 11:   *'Hangtown, gents! Looks mighty quiet today. Don't see nobody standin' under a pine limb with his boots off the ground.'*

Chapter 11:   *'Hang the cost, sir. We're celebrating our arrival. Bread and butter, if you please!'*

Chapter 12:   *'A woman like Miss Arabella marries a gentleman—not a butler. It simply isn't done. I wouldn't permit such a thing.'*

Chapter 13:   *'But I said ate—not eight.'*

Chapter 15:   *'Boy, the next time you point that squirrel gun at a bad hombre like me, you really ought to trouble yourself to reload it first.'*

Chapter 17:   *'Cut-Eye Higgins has done us a good turn—in spite of himself!'*

Chapter 18:   *(Azariah Jones) 'Me, I'd be doing fine if the rats don't put me out of the Cheap John business. Town's full of 'em. Why, a man can hardly stand still at night without something beginning to gnaw on his feet.'*

Conversations

Work in size-appropriate groups to write and perform the conversations that might have occurred in each of the following situations.

* Jack tells Aunt Arabella of his desire to go to the gold fields and strike it rich in order to help her save the family home. *(2 persons)*

* Captain Swain discovers Praiseworthy and Jack in the potato barrels before the ship leaves Boston. *(3 persons)*

* Captain Swain realizes that he is smoking rolled up money as he is talking with Jack and Praiseworthy. *(3 persons)*

* Captain Swain visits the captain of the *Sea Raven* after the *Lady Wilma* wins the race. *(2 persons)*

* Cut-Eye Higgins tells Praiseworthy and Jack how he found out that Good Luck was with him after he left the *Lady Wilma*. *(3 persons)*

* Jack has a conversation with Hanna, Quartz Jackson's new wife, and tells her it is difficult being so far away from his aunt. *(2 persons)*

* Praiseworthy tells Jack his true feelings about Aunt Arabella the day after they strike gold. *(2 persons)*

* Praiseworthy and Jack visit Cut-Eye Higgins in jail after they struck gold while digging the grave. *(3 persons)*

* After the fight with the Mountain Ox, Jack tells Praiseworthy how proud he was of the way the butler fought. *(2 persons)*

* Praiseworthy and Jack tell Dr. Buckbee that his map was worthless. *(3 persons)*

* Praiseworthy and Jack tell Aunt Arabella about how they lost their gold when the steamboat blew up. *(3 persons)*

* Aunt Arabella and Praiseworthy discuss what their life will be like after they get married. *(2 persons)*

* Praiseworthy talks to Jack the night before his wedding to Aunt Arabella. *(2 persons)*

Bibliography of Related Reading

Gold Rush

Andrist, Ralph. *The California Gold Rush.* (American Heritage Publishing, 1961)

Bauer, Helen. *California Gold Days.* (Doubleday, 1951)

Blumberg, Rhoda. *The American Gold Rush.* (Bradbury Press, 1989)

Gemming, Elizabeth. *Blow Ye Winds Westerly: The Seaports and Sailing Ships of Old New England.* (Harper, 1972)

Pack, Janet. *California.* (Watts, 1987)

Seidman, Laurence I. *Fools of '49.* (Knopf, 1976)

Stein, R. Conrad. *The Story of the Gold at Sutter's Mill.* (Children's, 1981)

Humorous Stories

Blume, Judy. *Starring Sally J. Freedman as Herself.* (Dell, 1977)

Byars, Betsy. *The Civil War.* (Scholastic, 1981)

Coren, Alan. *Arthur the Kid.* (Bantam, 1978)

Du Bois, William Pene. *Twenty-One Balloons.* (Penguin, 1947)

Elish, Dan. *The Worldwide Dessert Contest.* (Watts, 1988)

Feldman, Alan. *Lucy Mastermind.* (Dutton, 1985)

Fitzhugh, Louise. *Sport.* (Dell, 1979)

Fleischman, Sid. (Little, Brown and Company)

>   *Chancy and the Grand Rascal.* (1966)
>
>   *The Ghost on Saturday Night.* (1974)
>
>   *Humbug Mountain.* (1978)
>
>   *McBroom Tells the Truth.* (1981)
>
>   *Mr. Mysterious & Company.* (1962)

Hall, Lynn. *The Secret Life of Dagmar Schultz.* (Macmillan, 1988)

Jones, Rebecca C. *Germy Blew It.* (Dutton, 1987)

Lowry, Lois. *Anastasia Krupaik.* (Bantam, 1979)

Park, Barbara. *The Kid in the Red Jacket.* (Knopf, 1987)

Pinkwater, Daniel. *The Magic Moscow.* (Scholastic, 1980)

Rockwell, Thomas. *How to Eat Fried Worms.* (Dell, 1973)

Rodgers, Mary. *Freaky Friday.* (Harper, 1972)

Sharmat, Marjorie W. *Chasing After Annie.* (Harper, 1981)

Travels, P.L. *Mary Poppins.* (Scholastic, 1934)

Wolkoff, Judie. *In a Pig's Eye.* (Scholastic, 1977)

Other

Fleischman, Sid. *The Whipping Boy.* (Troll, 1986)

Sperry, Armstrong. *All Set Sail; A Romance of the Flying Cloud.* (Godine, 1982)

Answer Key Page

Page 11

1. Jack and Praiseworthy become stowaways because all their money is stolen.
2. Jack wants to become rich to help his Aunt Arabella and his sisters save their house and all their possessions from being sold.
3. If Captain Swain beats the other ship to San Francisco, he will become the captain of a brand new ship.
4. The Captain tells Praiseworthy he must shovel coal into the ship's boiler in order to pay for his fare.
5. Jack says he wants to work with Praiseworthy and shovel coal.
6. Praiseworthy puts coal dust on Good Luck and tells all the passengers to touch the pig. "Cut-Eye Higgins" refuses to and is left with clean hands.
7. The banknotes were found rolled up in cigars.
8. Accept appropriate answers.
9. The ship's first port of call will be Rio de Janeiro in Brazil.
10. The captain of the becalmed ship wants Captain Swain to pull them until their sails fill with wind. This takes five days.

Page 16

1. Accept appropriate summaries.
2. Jack was always worried that the cook would catch Good Luck and serve him for dinner.
3. Jack and Praiseworthy bought bananas, pineapples, and guavas.
4. Cut-Eye stole the gold map from Dr. Buckbee.
5. Cut-Eye unexpectedly took Good Luck with him. Jack was happy since he would no longer have to worry about the cook finding the pig.
6. The weather turned cold because as the ship moved south, it was further away from the equator.
7. In Tierra del Fuego the natives kept fires going day and night to keep themselves and their sheep from freezing.
8. Captain Swain took his ship through the Straits of Magellan to save several days of

travel and catch up with the *Sea Raven*.

9. Jack knew that there was moisture inside the potatoes so he suggested that the grape cuttings be put inside of them to keep them wet.
10. Praiseworthy told Captain Swain to burn the lumber that the ship was carrying to San Francisco.

Page 18

Latitude and Longitude

1. Los Angeles
2. San Francisco
3. San Diego
4. Santa Cruz
5. Fresno
6. Stockton
7. Barstow
8. Banning
9. Kings Canyon National Park
10. Lake Tahoe
11. Yosemite National Park
12. Death Valley National Monument

Page 21

1. Accept appropriate summaries.
2. It took so long to get shirts washed because the laundry sent them to China. It was cheaper to wash clothes there than in San Francisco.
3. Quartz Jackson tells Jack to save his whiskers because of the gold dust in them.
4. Accept appropriate answers. (Roaring Camp, Hangtown, Angels Camp, etc.) Jack wants to go to Hangtown.
5. Jack and Praiseworthy get one hundred dollars each for the pick and shovel.
6. The road agent means, put your hands up toward the sky or I will send you to heaven (the sky) by killing you.
7. Praiseworthy has Aunt Arabella's picture in his carpetbag.
8. Praiseworthy was able to knock the road agent fifteen feet because of the heavy gold dust in the fingertips of his glove.
9. In order to stake a claim, the miner pounds a peg in each of the four corners and puts a tin can on each peg.

Answer Key (cont.)

10. Pitch-pine Billy uses Praiseworthy's umbrella to pan for gold.

Page 26
1. Accept appropriate summaries.
2. The expression "takes a hair brush to you" means you will get a whipping with the backside of a hairbrush.
3. Praiseworthy doesn't think Miss Arabella would marry a butler because this would not be proper in the society of Boston.
4. The auctioneer hears Jack say "ate" and thinks he bid "eight" dollars for the neckties.
5. All the men want to be dressed up with a necktie to meet Quartz Jackson's new wife.
6. Praiseworthy knows he understands how to fight from reading a book about it. The Mountain Ox cannot read.
7. Jack and Praiseworthy find out from the miner that Cut-Eye is pretending to be a dentist in Shirt-Tale Camp.
8. Since Jack was being chased by an angry bear, it was fortunate he fell down the coyote hole.
9. Jack knows the man is one of the road agents who held them up because he is wearing Cut-Eye's coat.
10. Praiseworthy realizes that Cut-Eye must still have Dr. Buckbee's gold map.

Page 31
1. Accept appropriate summaries.
2. When the miner hits gold it will flatten out, but fool's gold will shatter.
3. Cut-Eye was being hanged for stealing a horse.
4. Jack and Praiseworthy discovered gold as they dug a grave for Cut-Eye.
5. Praiseworthy decided that the Mountain Ox's nose and jaw were his best targets.
6. The boiler on the steamboat exploded, sending Jack and Praiseworthy into the bay.
7. Jack and Praiseworthy let their gold fall because it was weighing them down, and they would have drowned.

8. Jack and Praiseworthy sold cats to all the merchants who were overrun with rats.
9. Aunt Arabella said she sold the house because it was a curse, full of musty old memories.
10. With Praiseworthy and Aunt Arabella getting married, Jack was going to have a real family at last.

Page 34
1. 4,000,000
2. a. 2,600,000 b. 450,000
4. 650,000
5. 200,000
6. 1,400,000
7. 850,000
8. OOOOOOOO
9. OOOOOOOOOOOO
10. 7,950,000

Page 43
Matching
1. Aunt Arabella
2. Mountain Ox
3. Captain Swain
4. Quartz Jackson
5. Cut-Eye Higgins
6. Praiseworthy
7. Pitch-pine Billy
8. Jack

True or False
1. True
2. False
3. False
4. True
5. True

Sequence
1-4-3-5-2

Page 44
Accept all reasonable responses.

Page 45
Perform the conversations (dramas) in class. Ask students to respond to the conversations in several different ways, such as, "Are the conversations realistic?" or "Are the words the characters say in keeping with their personalities?"